What Made the
GOOD
Samaritan
GOOD?

Awakening to
Life's Brutal Realities

MIKE HADDORFF | MIKE HAMEL

OTHER NONFICTION BOOKS
BY MIKE HAMEL

*The Entrepreneur's Creed: The Principles & Passions of
20 Successful Entrepreneurs*

Executive Influence: Impacting Your Workplace for Christ

Giving Back: Using Your Influence to Create Social Change

*Stumbling Toward Heaven: Mike Hamel on Cancer,
Crashes and Questions*

We Will Be Landing Shortly: Now What?

Spencer MacCallum: A Man Beyond His Time

Alvin Lowi Jr.: American Polymath

*Powering Social Enterprise with Profit and Purpose:
The Tandem Hybrid*

*Meeting Homelessness with HOPE: One Community's
Response*

Birth, Not Behavior: A Fresh Look at the Prodigal Son

What Made the
GOOD
Samaritan
GOOD?

Awakening to
Life's Brutal Realities

MIKE HADDORFF | MIKE HAMEL

This book is dedicated to:

Julie Briggs, the Best Samaritan I've ever known.
She cares for those left by the roadside,
from orphans and foster kids
to prisoners and victims of social injustice.
— Mike Hamel

Those of you attempting to
love others outside your box.
— Mike Haddorff

CONTENTS

In our first book, *Birth, Not Behavior: A Fresh Look At The Prodigal Son*, we took perhaps the most famous story Jesus told and brought it to life for modern readers. The central message of the parable is right there in our title: it is birth, not behavior—good or bad—that's the basis of God's unconditional love for all his children. In this book, we use perhaps his second most popular parable, the one about the Good Samaritan, to teach about the Brutal Realities of life.

Even those unfamiliar with the Bible have heard of the Prodigal Son and the Good Samaritan. But when Jesus first created these characters as heroes, it shocked his audience. A prodigal son did not deserve his father's love. A good Samaritan was an oxymoron, like "civil war" or "working vacation."

Jesus told his stories 2,000 years ago, but we still read and learn from them because they deal with key questions in life. They are as relevant today as when he first told him. The scenes he painted and the characters he created are still relational and relevant.

As in our first book, we use our imagination to bring the people in the parable to life. You'll meet Simeon the Scribe, an expert in the law who comes to Jesus with one of life's greatest questions: "What must I do to inherit eternal life?" As he often does, Jesus answers a question with a question, which leads to a discussion, which leads to a story. You'll meet Ephraim, a merchant from Samaria, and see what made him respond to a crisis like he did.

The title of this book asks: *What Made the Good Samaritan Good?* The answer is in the subtitle: *Awakening To Life's Brutal Realities.* We'll deal with four of these realities and show how to turn them from stumbling blocks into stepping stones.

INTRODUCTION

Almost everyone knows what a Good Samaritan is—someone who helps those in need, especially strangers. But in Jesus' day, it was a contradiction in terms. Samaritans were half-breeds, heretics, and enemies. To the Jews, a Samaritan was more likely to be the villain than the hero.

So, what made the Good Samaritan good?

Why does Jesus create this character in the first place?

What's the point of the parable Jesus makes up about him?

What are the takeaways for Jesus' audience then and now?

This book is our attempt to answer these and other questions.

In Chapter 1, you'll meet an expert in the law we call Simeon the Scribe. He asks Jesus a question most of us have asked at one time or another: "What must I do to inherit eternal life?" Many religious leaders tested Jesus with trick questions like, "Should we pay taxes to Caesar?" or, "If a woman was married to several men, which one would be her husband in heaven?" But Simeon is serious, which is why Jesus took him seriously.

Jesus gives an illustrative answer to this important question in story form. That's our focus in Chapter 2.

The protagonist of the provocative parable is a Samaritan merchant we call Ephraim. The setting is the road between Jerusalem and Jericho, a treacherous but vital trade route the Jews are familiar with. Finding a robbery victim on the side of the road wouldn't be unusual. A Samaritan helping such a victim would be.

In Chapters 3 and 5, we give Ephraim's backstory to explain why he acted the way he did. We suggest a history that illustrates what we call the four Brutal Realities of life. We look at them more in-depth in Chapters 4 and 6. Think of Chapters 3 and 5 as scenes in a movie. In Chapters 4 and 6, we, the screenwriters, talk to you, the readers, about the truths brought to life in the scenes.

We touched on the realities in our previous book, *Birth Not Behavior: A Fresh Look At the Prodigal Son*, where we wrote: "They lie in wait for everyone. If you draw breath, you will come across these truths sooner or later, regardless of race, gender, religion, or social status. . . . They are universal and unavoidable, although people experience them to different degrees and at different stages in life."

There's nothing new about these realities. Many teachers and writers have elaborated on them in their own way. Richard Rohr lists five in his book, *Adam's Return: The Five Promises of Male Initiation*: 1. Life is hard. 2. You are not important. 3. Your life is not about you. 4. You are not in control. 5. You are going to die.

Father Rohr refers to these as promises. We call them Brutal Realities because that's how they feel when they impact us. The adjective "brutal" isn't hyperbole. The word means "savage" or "cruel," and that's how they seem when they hit us. They can't be avoided, but if properly understood and dealt with, they can lead to growth and maturity.

For clarity, we number the realities and discuss them in order, but we don't experience them sequentially and separately. They are entwined in our daily experience.

Brutal Reality One: Life is hard. Hardships come in all forms: physical, spiritual, emotional, relational, financial, familial, etc. Hardships cause pain and suffering, and how we process them is crucial.

Brutal Reality Two: You are going to die. No surprise here. Most of us expect to die, just not in our lifetime. We write about the need to embrace our mortality because the degree to which we can do this is the degree to which we are free to live life to the fullest.

Brutal Reality Three: The world does not revolve around you. Our sense of identity and place in the world is defined by our personality, experiences, education, and culture. These often combine to tell us we don't deserve the attention we crave. But there's a healthier way to see ourselves that frees us to be who we are.

Brutal Reality Four: You are not in control. We try to maintain control by clamping down on the things and people around us, which puts us in a small box of our own making. We are meant for so much more but are afraid to let go and trust God. He invites us to step over the threshold of fear into the greater opportunities he has for us.

In Chapter 7, we speculate on what happened next. How does the answer Jesus gives to Simeon—go and do likewise—change his life? How is this admonition meant to change ours?

In the back of the book are discussion questions to help you dig deeper and draw out personal applications, plus some recommended resources and information about Christ In The Rockies. This program engages and encourages men in their masculine journey.

Wherever you are on your journey in life—a young person looking for direction, a businessperson striving to make a name for yourself, a mid-lifer searching for how to move from success to significance, or a senior eager to share your hard-earned wisdom with the next generation—you have faced these Brutal Realities in some form. May something in these pages help you accept and manage them in ways that make you more like the Good Samaritan.

1

Simeon's Question

On one occasion an expert in the law stood up to test Jesus. "Teacher," he asked, "what must I do to inherit eternal life?"

"What is written in the Law?" he replied. "How do you read it?"

He answered, "'Love the Lord your God with all your heart and with all your soul and with all your strength and with all your mind'; and, 'Love your neighbor as yourself.'"

"You have answered correctly," Jesus replied. "Do this and you will live."

But he wanted to justify himself, so he asked Jesus, "And who is my neighbor?"

Luke 10:25-29

A s a master storyteller, Jesus packs profound truths into simple tales. Like ants, his small stories carry several times their weight in meaning. With an economy of words, he paints vivid scenes and unforgettable characters to grab the emotions and call for a response. The story of the Good Samaritan is a prime example.

A question by an expert in the law prompts Jesus to tell this parable. We don't know much about the man except that he's probably a Pharisee since he asks about eternal life. Pharisees believed in the resurrection and life after death; the Sadducees and Essenes didn't. Today, Pharisees have a bad reputation as religious hypocrites in some circles. Back then, however, they were faithful conservatives who lived by the literal meaning of scripture. Some were rigid fundamentalists, while others were sincere believers trying to serve God.

We've given this legal scholar the name Simeon.

* * *

Simeon the Scribe came from the tribe of Levi and the town of Jericho. His father and grandfather were scribes. Simeon could read and write by the time he was five. He studied the twenty-four books of the Tanakh (the Jewish Bible) and memorized large portions of the Torah (the five books of Moses). After his apprenticeship, he moved to Jerusalem to study under Gamaliel the Elder, the grandson of Hillel.

Gamaliel was the leader of Beit Hillel, a prominent school of Pharisees. The Pharisees were one of three main Jewish sects, the others being the Sadducees and the Essenes. The word Pharisee means "one who is separated." It referred to their separation from unholy practices, undevout Jews, and Gentiles. In later years, the Talmud—the main text of rabbinic law and tradition—would list seven kinds of Pharisees, five of whom were criticized for their behavior. The two admired types of Pharisees were the "God-fearing" and the "God-loving." Simeon belonged to the latter group.

Mike Hamel: Some of the more zealous Pharisees were the fundamentalists of their day. Their devotion to God led to legalism. I'm a Former Fundie from the Jesus Revolution days. I didn't go to college because Jesus was coming back soon to rapture his church. That's the same reason I opted out of Social Security with a pastoral exemption and had no savings or retirement account. Health and life insurance were evidence of a lack of faith. God took care of the birds and flowers; he would take care of me.

I got up before dawn to read my Bible, the King James Version and interpreted it quite literally. That's why I spanked my kids (in love, not anger) and attended a church where the women weren't allowed to speak (1 Corinthians 14:34). I slept in a sleeping bag on the floor next to my bed to mortify the flesh. I went door-to-door to share the gospel and handed out tracks on street corners. I seldom spent a quarter on a soda because the money could be sent to missionaries in India. I alienated family and friends with my zeal, which only proved I was a true disciple.

What delivered me from fundamentalism was curiosity. Marketing guru Seth Godin makes a helpful distinction between the two in his book *Tribes*: "A fundamentalist is a person who considers whether a fact is acceptable to his religion before he explores it, as opposed to a curious person who explores first and then considers whether or not he wants to accept the ramifications. A curious person embraces the tension between his religion and something new, wrestles with it, through it, and then decides whether to embrace the new idea or reject it."

I believe curiosity comes from being made in God's image. If he weren't curious, we wouldn't be here. I believe asking questions is not a sin, even if we sometimes come up with wrong answers. I believe changing our minds can be a sign of gullibility or maturity and that it takes some of the former to acquire the latter.

Simeon studied hard and became well-respected among his peers. He married and had two sons who joined him in the family business after completing their apprenticeship as scribes. He taught in the synagogue, and his lectures in the Temple precincts were very popular. He loved the Lord and his law and could expound on it in three languages: Hebrew, Aramaic, and Greek.

The high point in his life was his selection to the Great Sanhedrin, the official judiciary for the Jews. His appointment was aided by his being a Levite, a Pharisee, and a noted legal scholar. Knowledge of the Torah wasn't enough, however; judges had to know something about other fields like medicine, mathematics, astronomy, and pagan religions so they could deal with cases involving these subjects.

After his appointment, Simeon turned his business over to his sons and taught fulltime, gathering a growing cohort of students. They were the ones who first told him about John the Baptizer. Simeon went to the Jordan River to hear the fiery preacher. He marveled at the multitudes who heeded John's message and were baptized. Later, he heard a cousin of John's, Jesus of Nazareth, had started an itinerant ministry with a few of John's disciples.

Rumors started coming in from Galilee, Capernaum, and the Decapolis about this new prophet who drew even bigger crowds than John. Jesus taught the masses who lived in the countryside and didn't have access to the scholars and scribes in Jerusalem. That wasn't all he did. There were startling reports of miracles, with enough credible witnesses that the stories couldn't be easily dismissed.

One day, his friend Nicodemus told Simeon of an unsettling conversation he'd had with Jesus. "When we spoke about the Kingdom of God," Nicodemus said, "he told me one had to be born of the spirit to enter it. When I asked what that meant, he scolded me for not understanding heavenly things. He spoke of the Son of Man being lifted up just as Moses lifted up the snake in the wilderness and that those who believed in him would have eternal life."

Simeon frowned. Eternal life was an important topic for the Pharisees. Who was this Galilean to claim he could bestow it?

"We know of the Son of Man from the prophet Daniel," Nicodemus went on, "but I'm not sure what he meant by the reference to Moses."

His curiosity—and anger—aroused, Simeon went looking for the controversial young rabbi. He found him teaching a large crowd. It was easy to see what drew them. Despite his lack of formal training, Jesus was a mesmerizing teacher. Unlike other popular preachers and self-proclaimed messiahs, he didn't have a political agenda. He didn't incite rebellion against Rome. He talked about love and caring for the poor. He respected the law but had some unorthodox interpretations.

Simeon loved the law and had mixed feelings about how Jesus handled it. What did Jesus think about the weightier matters like eternal life? As a Pharisee,

Simeon believed in the resurrection and an afterlife where people would be rewarded for righteousness or punished for wickedness. How you lived now determined your place in David's restored kingdom, which the Messiah would usher in.

The Sadducees believed none of this. The grave was the end for them.

What did Jesus believe? Simeon wondered. He decided to find out. He worked his way to the front of the crowd and got the chance to ask his question.

As he often did, Jesus responded with questions of his own: "What is written in the Law? How do you read it?"

Without hesitation, Simeon replied, "Love the Lord your God with all your heart and with all your soul and with all your strength and with all your mind, and love your neighbor as yourself."

"You have answered correctly," Jesus replied. "Do this and you will live."

Simeon agreed with the first part. He felt the entire Law of Moses could be summarized in two brief commands: love God and love your neighbor as yourself. But doing it wasn't so easy. For centuries the Jews wrestled with the details of obeying the law. The simple command to keep the Sabbath had to be clarified by the thirty-nine kinds of work prohibited on that day. The Torah told Israel to pay tithes, but there were first, second, and third tithes to be sorted out. Some went to the Levites, some to the priests, and some to the poor. Obedience was complicated, but earning eternal life in the future depended on living a holy life in the present.

Simeon also believed the term "neighbor" didn't apply to everyone. The verses he quoted to Jesus, Leviticus 19:17-18, clearly applied to fellow Jews. In the Torah, it says "You shall not hate *your brother* in your heart; you shall reprove *your kinsman*, and not incur guilt because of him. You shall not take vengeance or bear a grudge against any of *your people*, but you shall love your neighbor like yourself; I am YHWH." The word "neighbor" used here meant "friend" or "associate." That's how the Pharisees interpreted it and why they only used the term with each other in their tight-knit community.

Fast forward to today. We aren't so different from the Pharisees, as Timothy Keller points out: "We instinctively tend to limit for whom we exert ourselves. We do it for people like us, and for people whom we like. Jesus will have none of that. By depicting a Samaritan helping a Jew, Jesus could not have found a more forceful way to say that anyone in need—regardless of race, politics, class, and religion—is your neighbour. Not everyone is your brother or sister in faith, but everyone is your neighbour, and you must love your neighbour."

Mike Haddorff: Earlier in life, I would've made a pretty good Pharisee with my sense of religious superiority. There was a judgmental aspect to my character from the start. I felt put in a position of responsibility as the firstborn son, and I took that seriously. I can remember thinking if Dad just straightened up, life would be so much better. Looking back, I've often wished I had treated others with less judgment and more compassion, especially those nearest and dearest to me.

My early Christian experience reinforced this Pharisaical bent. I saw the Bible as God's instruction book, and if you didn't measure up, too bad for you. I attended the Discipleship Intern Training Program in the 1970s where we were taught that if we met someone who was struggling, we were to give them scripture to memorize, a book to read, and ask them to write a report. Then we were to set up a meeting to review the report. I mean, how legalistic is that? I treated all my relationships the same way, expecting others to straighten up and do what God said and judging them when they didn't measure up.

I've dramatically changed over the years. I've realized I hurt family and friends, and to the best of my ability, I've gone back and made amends where I could. But even at age seventy, there's still a bit of the Pharisee in me. It's not who I want to be, and I deeply admire the Samaritan we are talking about in this book and how he was moved by compassion instead of a judgmental spirit, as were the priest and Levite.

Jesus is teaching an absolute truth in this parable—compassion is more important than anything else.

Simeon couldn't let Jesus' broader definition of neighbor go unchallenged, so he asked another question.

"And who is my neighbor?"

2

Jesus'
Answer

In reply Jesus said: "A man was going down from Jerusalem to Jericho, when he was attacked by robbers. They stripped him of his clothes, beat him and went away, leaving him half dead. A priest happened to be going down the same road, and when he saw the man, he passed by on the other side. So too, a Levite, when he came to the place and saw him, passed by on the other side. But a Samaritan, as he traveled, came where the man was; and when he saw him, he took pity on him. He went to him and bandaged his wounds, pouring on oil and wine. Then he put the man on his own donkey, brought him to an inn and took care of him. The next day he took out two denarii and gave them to the innkeeper. 'Look after him,' he said, 'and when I return, I will reimburse you for any extra expense you may have.'

"Which of these three do you think was a neighbor to the man who fell into the hands of robbers?"

The expert in the law replied, "The one who had mercy on him."

Jesus told him, "Go and do likewise."

Luke 10:30-37

Now we come to the parable of the Good Samaritan itself. Often, Jesus' parables were enigmatic and provocative. This isn't one of those obscure parables. The meaning is right there on the surface: A good neighbor is someone who helps those in need. Be a good neighbor.

There are three actors in this little drama: a priest, a Levite, and a Samaritan. Jews typically classified themselves as priests, Levites, and Israelites. For Jesus to switch Israelite to Samaritan—their mortal enemies—caught his audience completely off guard. It was like preaching a sermon on The Good Muslim in New York City the Sunday after 9/11.

Jesus' unlikely hero is a Samaritan we call Ephraim.

* * *

This parable comes in answer to a series of questions:

"What must I do to inherit eternal life?"

"What is written in the Law. How do you read it?"

"Who is my neighbor?"

Jesus wasn't trying to win an argument with a legal scholar. His answers weren't aimed at the head but at the heart and hands. They came in the form of a morality tale. Jesus wanted to move the expert and the listening audience to compassionate action. He wanted to bring the subject of eternal life into the here and now.

Jesus chose a dangerous setting for his story: the Jericho Road. This busy trade route descended almost 3,500 feet from Jerusalem in the mountains to Jericho by the Dead Sea. The steep passes, blind turns, and desert terrain made it Ambush Alley for bandits and robbers, so much so that it was known at the time as The Way of Blood.

Given the location, it would be tragic but not surprising to find a man "attacked by robbers. They stripped him of his clothes, beat him and went away, leaving him half dead."

Nor would it be surprising that a priest succumbed to the Bystander Effect and "passed by on the other side." Perhaps he felt he had to keep himself ritually clean for service in the Temple. He couldn't tell if the man in the ditch was dead or alive. If he touched a corpse, he would have to go through a seven-day cleansing ritual before he could perform his sacred duties.

If this was his reasoning, it was a sham. As a priest, he knew the Mishnah, the oral law. It clearly taught that saving a life trumped all other laws. And if the man were dead, the law required even the high priest to tend to a neglected corpse. To use the law to sidestep the law is the epitome of hypocrisy.

What could be said of the priest could also be said of the Levite, a fellow religious professional. He also chose to ignore his duty.

Before we get too judgmental, let's admit many of us have acted the same way on occasion. How often have we switched sides of the street to avoid a homeless person or driven by a car on the side of the road with the hood up? We tell ourselves: *"Someone else will stop." "I'm late for an appointment." "It might not be safe."* But are these reasons—or excuses?

Mike Haddorff: Why didn't the priest and Levite respond with compassion to the robbery victim? Perhaps they were more concerned with staying clean than showing compassion. I can relate.

As I think about my early days in the Vineyard, what drew me to the movement was the emphasis on praying for and ministering to others. We entered into their pain in a personal way. I liked that approach, as opposed to my time with the Brethren, where the way you ministered to people was to teach them the Word.

When you enter into the pain of others, you encounter their unfortunate circumstances. Your empathy opens you up to their hurt, discouragement, or depression. In the Vineyard, we had a term for this. We called it getting slimed. The term came from the old Ghostbuster movie where the heroes got slimed when fighting the ghosts.

We used it to define getting something negative from the person we ministered to.

After getting slimed, the idea was to receive cleansing prayer to restore emotional balance. It wasn't as simple as that, but you get the point. There had to be a way to get free from the taint of what affected those we were helping. This reflects the idea of clean and unclean, which is part of the natural way we think. So, even when motivated by compassion, we still had to deal with getting clean.

To put this in an elementary school metaphor, some people had cooties, and when you touched them, you got cooties, which wasn't cool. As one comic put it, "Of all the things I learned in grade school, avoiding cooties was the last thing I expected to be the most useful."

Slime, cooties, unclean, they all mean the same thing, being contaminated by others. This is something we naturally avoid, but compassion overcomes this by putting others first.

Now, here's the surprising part. The man who cared for the victim was a Samaritan. That's like a member of the Ku Klux Klan stopping to help an injured black man in Mississippi in the 1920s. Unexpected, to say the least. Especially for a Jewish audience, for whom Samaritans were even lower than Gentiles, being half-breeds and heretics. The worst insult a Jew could hurl at someone was to call him a Samaritan.

Jews and Samaritans were bitter enemies; their animosity went back centuries.

When the northern kingdom of Israel was conquered in 721 BCE, the Assyrians deported the cream of society and replaced them with foreigners. The commoners who remained and intermarried with the outsiders became known as Samaritans. A few centuries later, when the Jews returned under Ezra and Nehemiah to rebuild Jerusalem and the Temple, the Samaritans opposed them and tried to sabotage their efforts.

The Samaritans had never left the Holy Land and saw themselves as the true Jews. They were descendants of the tribes of Ephraim and Manasseh. They had the original version of the Torah, not the corrupted version possessed by the other tribes. They rejected the illegitimate temple and priesthood based in Jerusalem and worshipped on Mount Gerizim, the Mount of Blessing, where Moses told half the Israelites to stand during the reading of the law (Deuteronomy 11:29).

The Jews saw things differently. God told his people not to intermarry with the people of the lands he gave them; the Samaritans did just that. God told his people to worship only at the Temple in Jerusalem; the Samaritans built their temple on Mount Gerizim. God gave his people the twenty-four books of the Tanak; the Samaritans rejected the books of poetry and prophecy and had their version of the Torah.

Samaria was on the wrong side of the tracks as far
as the Jews were concerned, and they avoided it whenever possible. Devout Jews crossed the Jordan River
rather than go through Samaria. But Jews and Samaritans couldn't avoid one another on the Jericho Road.

Ephraim was one such Samaritan who knew the
Jericho Road. He was the second son of a prosperous
merchant based in Jericho. His older brother lived in
the seaport city of Joppa and handled the shipping end
of the business. The family imported exotic goods from
far-off lands, such as spices, oils, perfumes, ivory, and
silk. They exported dates, olives, and wool. Ephraim
was the main conduit between the two markets.

Business was good, but that hadn't always been the
case. Ephraim had his share of struggles and setbacks.
Given the value of his merchandise, he'd been attacked
and robbed before. His wife begged him to get off the
road, but his father insisted he stay personally involved
with their customers. This was easier to do in Samaria
among his brethren than in Jerusalem, where he had to
work through middlemen the Jews would accept.

Ephraim understood the tension between Samaritans
and Jews. He was religious but not a fanatic. He judged
people by their behavior, not their background. In his years
on the road, he'd seen the best and worst of folks, and the
labels they wore didn't make much difference. His creed
was to treat others the way he wanted to be treated.

That's why when he saw the man in the ditch, Ephraim didn't hesitate to help. "He went to him and bandaged his wounds, pouring on oil and wine. Then he put the man on his own donkey, brought him to an inn and took care of him." That's acute care.

"The next day, he took out two denarii and gave them to the innkeeper. 'Look after him,' he said." That's financial care.

"And when I return, I will reimburse you for any extra expense you may have." That's comprehensive care.

Jesus made a hated enemy the hero to drive home a point even the Jewish expert recognized. When Jesus asked, "Which of these three do you think was a neighbor to the man who fell into the hands of robbers?" the expert in the law replied, "The one who had mercy on him." He couldn't bring himself to say Samaritan.

This was admitting that even enemies should be neighbors. It was saying compassion was more important than religious distinctions.

Mike Hamel: What I get out of this parable are some guidelines for whom NOT to help. In the age of 24/7 news, I hear about every disaster from everywhere every day. The injustices and suffering bring me to tears at times. I wish I could help every hungry child, every abused woman, every crime victim, every homeless person. But I can't. I have limited resources and commitments I can barely keep up with. Who is MY neighbor when it comes to hands-on involvement? Based on this parable, MY neighbor is:

1. Someone I meet personally. This includes family, friends, and some strangers I meet who have needs others don't know about or aren't meeting.
2. Someone the Spirit prompts me to help. Not even Jesus met every need. He didn't heal everyone or raise all his friends who died. He listened for his Father's direction on what to do.
3. Someone whose immediate needs I can meet with my gifts and resources. The Samaritan used what he had at the time to address the victim's current and short-term needs.
4. Someone who doesn't have to pay me back. The Samaritan put no conditions on his aid and didn't expect a return. Jesus healed people based on their needs, not on how they might respond.

I don't mean to imply we shouldn't support larger causes. I've invested time and money in people, churches, and ministries beyond my direct experience. But even this is based on a sense of personal calling. I can't do everything, but I can do something. My friend Jack Briggs, former CEO of Springs Rescue Mission, puts it this way: "Don't try to change the world; you aren't equipped for that. But here's what you can do. Be a positive influence in the three feet around you all day long. If you positively influence the things and people within your span of influence, the ripple effect from that three feet can travel a long way."

Martin Luther King, Jr. once observed, "The first question which the priest and the Levite asked was: 'If I stop to help this man, what will happen to me?' But . . . the good Samaritan reversed the question: 'If I do not stop to help this man, what will happen to him?'"

Jesus didn't mention what made the Samaritan the kind of man who responded the way he did. What produced his compassionate concern for others?

That's a good question.

Read on for a plausible answer.

3

Ephraim's Story
Part 1

"Which of these three do you think was a neighbor
to the man who fell into the hands of robbers?"

The expert in the law replied, "The one who
had mercy on him."

Luke 10:36-37

"Some stories are true that never happened," wrote
Elie Wiesel. Jesus told stories that never happened,
with characters who never existed, to teach truths about
real life. We've created backstories for his characters
for the same reason. When thinking about what might
have made Ephraim become the Good Samaritan, let's
start with a question: Why do some people turn away
from an accident while others rush to help? Tempera-
ment plays a part, but so does experience. Those who
have experienced pain and suffering are more likely to
show mercy and compassion.

Pain and suffering are often caused by what we call
the four Brutal Realities: Life is hard, You are going to

die, The world does not revolve around you, You are not in control. They come in various forms and at different times but are common to all humans. Let's consider how Ephraim might have experienced the first two.

* * *

Ephraim was good with numbers and even better with people, which served him well as a merchant. Not that he had a choice in careers. His grandfather Akabon had started the trading business his father Yaakov now ran. Ephraim's older brother, Nathan, was as driven as their father and hence his favorite son.

Ephraim enjoyed his work but couldn't keep up with his brother, no matter how much he tried. Nathan sat in the trading house in Joppa, where merchants from many lands came to barter. Ephraim was on the road dealing with the provincials in Judea, the Galilee, and Samaria. Business went smoother in Samaria among his brethren than in Judea among the Jews. The animosity between the races was always in the air.

The Jews only tolerated him because of the quality of his goods. They insulted him and tried to swindle him whenever they could. He deflected this mistreatment with humor. He made himself the butt of his own jokes and sunk as low as it took to make the sale. But on the inside, he was fuming.

Stuffing his anger affected his relationships at home. It made him short-tempered and sullen. His mood worsened whenever he had to report to his father, who constantly pressured him to generate more revenue. "If you did half as well at selling as your brother and I do at buying, we would be so much better off," Yaakov often told him. This deflated Ephraim, but he didn't have other options.

Being on the road brought its own kind of pressure. Travel was inconvenient at best and perilous at worst. Crude inns or cold nights under the stars were his only choices for lodging. He was plagued by irate customers, dishonest tax collectors, and thieving soldiers who took what they wanted on their way past his donkeys, tapping the handles of their swords to silence any protests.

Ephraim joined trading caravans with armed guards when he could. Otherwise, he was by himself. He was alone one fall day going up the Ascent of Adummim on the Jericho Road when his life changed forever.

It almost ended forever.

His donkey was having trouble pulling an overloaded cart up the steep incline when a snake slithered onto the road and startled the poor beast. It bolted left and tipped over the cart, which fell on Ephraim, breaking his leg and pinning him to the ground. He went in and out of consciousness over the next few hours. If bandits had found him, they would have looted his wares and left him for dead. Fortunately, a date farmer and his two sons came along. They freed Ephraim and took him and his cart to their farm, which was closer than any town. They brought out a physician to set his broken leg and, a few days later, took him home to Jericho.

Mike Haddorff: I had an accident a few years ago where I received a blow to the back of my head. I went to bed as usual but woke up at 4:30 a.m. when I could feel something happening. I didn't know it at the time, but the blow created a blood clot that came loose and caused a stroke.

I felt dizzy and knew something was wrong. I got up and was very disoriented. I made it to the sink in my bathroom and threw up. My wife, Sandra, was out of town, and my son, Mike, was in our guest bedroom. I had to feel my way down the hall to wake him and tell him what was happening. He called an ambulance and the paramedics quickly arrived. I threw up a few more times while we waited.

As they wheeled me out, I said to one of them, "I may have had a stroke."

He said, "You may be right."

I spent the morning in the ER throwing up and undergoing various tests. I felt terrible. Everything was out of whack. That evening, the neurologist confirmed I'd had a stroke. They monitored me for the next few days and gave me drugs to get the nausea under control, but I still felt on the verge of throwing up all the time.

I was seeing double. I saw two clocks on the wall where there was only one. My family was in the dark; they thought I might be dying. I vaguely remember them coming into the room. I knew they were there, but I couldn't respond, and, honestly, I just didn't care. I just wanted to be left alone.

By days three and four, I started to improve. The two clocks on the wall began to merge into one. I was able to walk and do some physical therapy. A funny aside: one of the rehab staff was a beautiful young woman. I remember saying to her, "You are absolutely beautiful, but you have three eyes."

A week or so later, I was released under ongoing medical care. I couldn't drive for a month, but most things returned to normal.

I liken my experience to the accident we've imagined for Ephraim. All I was aware of was the pain of being pinned down and disoriented. I had no control over my circumstances. I was trapped in a terrible and painful "present." I was oblivious to the future or the possibility of dying; I just didn't care.

I look back and am so thankful for the help I received and that my accident wasn't fatal. This brush with mortality made me more thankful for life and for being able to do the normal things I used to take for granted.

Johanna was beside herself with gratitude when she saw her husband. Ephraim was five days late, and given the dangers of the road, she didn't know if he was dead or alive. "What happened!" she exclaimed.

Ephraim told her about the accident and the kindness of Abner and his sons.

"The physician said your man should make a full recovery," Abner assured her. "The break was clean."

"Let me pay you for your time and trouble," Ephraim offered. "Johanna, get my strongbox."

"No need," Abner said.

"At least let us pay for the physician," Johanna said.

Abner shook his head. "We all need help sometimes. My father used to say, 'Kindness is freely given.'"

Johanna put Ephraim to bed for some much needed rest. The next day, he sent word to his father about the accident. Yaakov showed up a week later.

When Ephraim described his ordeal and pointed to his broken leg, Yaakov shrugged. "I'm sorry this happened, but I need you. When you can get around on crutches, there are two wagons of dates that must go to Joppa. Hire some help, but get them there by the end of the month."

This was the level of sympathy Ephraim expected. His father was a tough man who showed little emotion.

"He shouldn't have to work alone," Johanna said. "It's too dangerous."

"Then he can stay home," Yaakov said. "I'll get someone else."

"No, no," Ephraim spoke. "I'll see to it."

"Your father doesn't respect how hard you work," Johanna said after Yaakov left.

"He's always been demanding," Ephraim said. "But he's still my father. He's given me all I have in life. If only he gave me more credit for what I do."

"Maybe you should stop trying to please him and do something else," Johanna said.

"Like what? I love trading and bartering, and I'm good at it."

"Do it in town where it's safer, " Johanna pleaded.

"You heard my father. He wants me back on the road. I don't have enough saved to defy him."

"Then, when you go to Joppa, do me a favor."

"What?"

"Go up and see your Uncle Mordecai. He's dealt with your father longer than you have. Ask him for advice."

Mordecai was Yaakov's younger brother. The two had worked together for many years before Mordecai started his own business in Apollonia, just up the coast from Joppa.

"I'll think about it," Ephraim said.

Three days later, Ephraim collected the dates and hired a former soldier as a helper. When he passed over the Ascent of Adummim, he stopped where he'd lain helpless for several hours. The rust-colored stain on the road was his blood. He could have died there if not for the kindness of strangers.

The trip to Joppa was without incident, but it unnerved Ephraim enough to take Johanna's advice and visit his uncle.

"My favorite nephew!" Mordecai greeted him with a bear hug. "What's with the crutches?"

Ephraim told him about the accident, then added. "Johanna wants me to do something safer."

"What would you do?"

"I could take up fishing or farming, anything to get me off the road."

Mordecai frowned. "You are a broker to your bones. Why change?"

"To not die?"

Mordecai put his arm around Ephraim's shoulder. "Walk with me. I'll take it slow."

He guided his nephew to his favorite trail running along the coast within the sound of the waves. After several minutes of silence, Mordecai said, "I know what you feel. When I was still with Yaakov, we were shipwrecked off the coast of Africa and several of our crew drowned. A year later, I was wounded in a brawl with some Galileans over who should pay the tax on a catch of fish."

"I was very young, but I remember the shipwreck," Ephraim said. "I never heard about the brawl."

Mordecai stopped and took off his sandals. He held up his left foot. It was missing the little toe. He smiled. "That story takes longer to tell. So does this one." He pulled up his sleeve to reveal a jagged scar on his right forearm. "The longer we live, the more pain we will have. The more scars we will acquire." He pointed at Ephraim's leg. "Life-threatening experiences like my shipwreck and your accident cause us to face our mortality. At such times, we have a choice."

"Yeah," Ephraim said. "Choose a safer career."

Mordecai chuckled. "You can't escape that easily. Fishermen face empty nets and fierce storms. Some drown. Farmers live through drought and pestilence. Any path you choose will be like the road to Jericho in its own way. Your choice is what to do about the dangers. You can either try to ignore them or accept them."

"Ignoring them seems wiser," Ephraim said.

"Is it? You know who chose that option?"

"Who?"

"Your father."

Ephraim stopped walking. "I need a rest. These crutches are killing my armpits. Now, what about my father?"

They found a perch on a flat rock. "Yaakov went through the same troubles as me, and more," Mordecai said." Rather than bend like a branch in the wind, he dug his roots down deep. He determined never to be

45

defeated. He would control everything and everyone around him. He would take the pain without flinching and challenge death to either give way or take him out. You know the kind of man it made him. Hard. Demanding of himself and others. Do you want to end up like that?"

Ephraim cringed. He did not want to become his father. At the same time, he didn't want to wind up roadkill. "So, I just expect to be at risk all the time?"

"In our business, yes," Mordecai replied. I had to come to grips with that. I could either turn away from what I loved or include the negative that came with it. I moved ahead and started my own business."

"Were you afraid of failing?"

"Terrified. But I figured little risk, little reward. It was a struggle at first, and your father didn't help. He resented my competition."

"Sounds like him," Ephraim said.

"I'm not suggesting you be foolish or passive," Mordecai said. "Be prepared. Weigh the risks. Use your brain. Plan ahead. And part of wise planning is accepting what you can't control or change. Accidents happen. Minimize the danger all you can, but avoiding it altogether is impossible. Accept it, and don't let fear keep you from living."

That made sense to Ephraim. It didn't mean it would be easy to do, though.

"One more thing," Mordecai said as he stood and turned toward town. "You have abilities you should not waste. Don't let what might happen keep you from who you are meant to be."

"I would like to be my own man," Ephraim said. "But what if I fail?"

"Then try again," Mordecai urged. "Follow your heart and see what happens. There's no time like the present; we don't know what tomorrow will bring." He pointed at the surf as they walked. "Our livelihood comes to us over those waves. Shipments are scheduled and sent, but there are always setbacks. Nothing is certain. Make your plans, then do your best with what the tide brings."

Mike Hamel: There are events that cause trouble and discomfort that we somehow manage to get through. Then there are seasons when everything goes sideways and stays that way for a long time. I had one such ten-year stretch that reshaped my thinking about God, the world, and everything in it.

In the spring of 2007, an online company I wrote for went bankrupt, and I filed for unemployment for the first time. Shortly after, I was diagnosed with non-Hodgkin's lymphoma, and I didn't have health insurance. I went through six rounds of chemo, but the cancer returned, so I underwent a bone marrow transplant in 2008. Ten weeks later, I was in a serious auto accident resulting in a broken back, fractured sternum, cracked ribs, and torn rotator cuffs in both shoulders.

The extensive chemo I went through for my bone marrow transplant gave me another cancer, squamous cell carcinoma, for which I had surgery, extensive radiation, and more chemo. No sooner had I finished my last chemo treatment than my wife of thirty-seven years died of a sudden heart attack on Thanksgiving 2011.

In 2016, my lymphoma returned, and I had a second bone marrow transplant. The chances of survival were less than 20%. After only eleven weeks, the lymphoma returned, leading to another surgery and more chemo.

This isn't all that happened during that decade, but you get the picture. I wrote about it in my book, *We Will be Landing Shortly: Now What?*:

> Given my hardships, some friends have compared me to Job. That's quite a stretch. Job was very wealthy; I'm a freelance writer with no set income. Job had vast herds and holdings; I don't even own a dog. Job was known and respected in heaven; I doubt my name comes up there very often. . . . What Job and I have in common is a concentrated period of suffering and loss leading to a sense of alienation from God. . . . Despite being

confused and angry about our circumstances, neither of us cursed God nor doubted his existence. Eventually, Job was restored to fellowship, not by anything he did but simply by God showing up. Job wasn't revived by the answers he got to his questions—God didn't bother. Nor was it the outpouring of physical blessings—those came later. His transformation was sparked by God's tangible presence.

I longed for a sense of God's presence but didn't feel it, which was perhaps the most difficult hardship of all. What has changed over the years since then is my perception of who God is and how he speaks.

4

Brutal Realities
One and Two

In the previous Chapter, Ephraim encountered Brutal Realities One and Two. Life was hard because of the pressure his father put on him and the struggle to make a living in a hostile environment. It became harder after his accident. He came face to face with his mortality, and it shook him to his core.

Ephraim's wife, Johanna, and Uncle Mordecai helped him process his pain. Mordecai encouraged him to accept the negative events in life and to see himself and his circumstances differently. His default settings needed adjustment.

Here's what we would tell Ephraim and his counterparts today.

* * *

Every human being has a default way of responding to any given situation. Our default setting is influenced by our family background, religious training, and early life experiences. It's natural and, unfortunately, limited, especially when it comes to how we handle the hard things in life. This brings us to the first Brutal Reality: Life is hard. We experience this hardness as pain. Pain is unavoidable. "Pain is the rent we pay for being human," notes Richard Rohr, "but suffering is usually optional."

Every child experiences some level of wounding. It can be physical pain caused by an external source or emotional pain caused by participation in events that violate our sense of right and wrong. A hard punch in the gut causes physical pain. Sneaking a peek at your father's *Playboy* (we grew up before the internet, remember) causes feelings of shame and guilt.

As children, we don't have the tools to process pain, which creates all kinds of turmoil we don't know how to deal with. Whose fault is it? What should we do with this pain, guilt, and confusion? Should we lash back? Will that get rid of it? We look to adults, usually our parents, for clues. Often, they are positive role models, but sometimes their examples are negative.

We process both types of pain on conscious and subconscious levels. Picture the levels as the main floor and the basement of a house. What often happens is we stuff our pain down into the basement. If the experience is especially hurtful, we cram it in a box, tape it shut, and hide it in a corner. It must be gone, so we think. The truth is, it's still there, dormant but unresolved.

Mike Haddorff: My family lived in Southern California when I was four. My parents had property with two small houses in the front and a duplex in the back where we lived. Next door was the Hollisters' large two-story house. Their son, Scott, was my age. Mr. Hollister put in an in-ground swimming pool and built a six-foot wooden fence between our yards for safety reasons.

Scott made it clear in a four-year-old way that this was his pool. He told me several times I couldn't swim in it. This was new to me. I'd never heard, "You can't." Being an only child, my world was, "You cute little guy; you can have whatever you want." Hearing, "You can't," pissed me off before I knew what being pissed off meant. "What do you mean I can't?"

I could understand Scott being king of the pool. But if the king says, "You can't," I will do all I can to make his life miserable. *Side note: I marvel at how this strategy solidified in my head. Throughout my life, I've tried to "Make the king miserable" on numerous occasions. It's never worked.*

I'll show you who's king. I pulled my little red wagon into position, stabilizing it against the fence. I put my tricycle onto the deck of the wagon. I found dirt clods and rocks, climbed up on my engineering marvel, and hurled my wrath over the fence.

In absolute delight, I heard my bombs crash onto the deck. An occasional splash meant a direct hit! I remember scrounging up a piece of old tricycle tire as my prized projectile. After a few moments of bombing ecstasy, I dismantled my launching apparatus.

That evening, I was in my bedroom and heard a knock on the front door. I heard Mr. Hollister talking to my dad. I could guess what it was about. Then my dad walked calmly into my room and asked if I had done what Mr. Hollister said. *Side note: My second marvel is how well I've perfected lying for self-preservation. It took decades of practice, but I've mastered the art of lying to myself and others, even in the face of the absolutely obvious.*

"No, I don't know what he's talking about."

I don't remember any discipline. I think my dad felt sorry for me.

I also don't remember ever swimming in the pool. There's probably some deep-seated unresolved wound connected to that. What I do remember is this was the first time I experienced woundedness, and my way of getting back was causing hurt because I'd been hurt.

Life goes on; we grow up. Something painful happens that scrapes the unresolved wound and we react. Maybe we shut down, or we fly off the handle. We ask, "Where did that come from?" Because we feel pain, we handle it the way we learned to as kids. This is our default mode. Recall when you were a child; how was pain processed in your immediate surroundings? Do you find yourself reacting similarly today?

There's another way of seeing reality and processing pain. In Philippians, the Apostle Paul speaks about a different way of thinking, which he calls the mind of Christ. How did Jesus deal with pain? He was certainly no stranger to it. Studying his life, we see how he transformed pain by facing it. Think of his agony-ridden monologue in the garden. He's alone, trembling in the face of what's about to occur, yet he gasps, "Father, not my will but yours be done."

Facing pain means bringing it out of the basement into the light of day. It's admitting that ignoring, numbing, or blaming others isn't working. It's finding the box in the corner and tearing off the tape. There are unresolved wounds inside, but now they're out in the open and can start to heal.

If there's a first significant step, it's when we decide enough is enough. We're sick and tired of being sick and tired. There's no way around it, only through it. Choosing "through" doesn't mean it's instantly fixed; it just means the box is now in the open and healing can occur because it's in the light.

From this first major move, let me (Mike Haddorff) suggest how to transform pain in four general steps:

Include: By this, I mean include the negative, which means accepting it as something that's true. It might involve standing before a group of strangers and saying, "Hi, my name is Glen, and I'm an alcoholic." Or admitting to a spouse, "Yes, I did spend our savings on gambling." Whatever the wound and resulting pain, we must accept it as true before we can be transformed. Our old methods of denial, numbing, or blaming haven't worked. Only through inclusion can change begin. As the humorist Ashleigh Brilliant says, "If you can't go around it, over it, or through it, you had better negotiate with it."

Connect: Remember the Connect-The-Dots drawings we used to do as kids? Dozens of dots meant nothing until you connected them into a picture. Once we include the negative as part of the picture, we can start connecting ALL the existing dots. Prior to this, there was no accurate picture because many dots were missing. Only now can we see all the components of the big picture instead of just the things we want to see. We can see the connections between our upbringing, our relationships, or lack thereof, and, to some degree, our thinking. We start to understand the why.

This broader perspective is something we're now able to feel, and the feeling is good. It becomes recognizable as freedom. This is how we can tell our awareness is expanding beyond the box we've been living in. Robert Frost once asked: "How many things have to happen to you before something occurs to you?" Enough has happened to make us awake and aware.

Grieve: We need a mechanism to deal with the pain that results from accepting reality, a way to face the ugliness. It's the healing role of grief. We can't change what has occurred, but we can receive healing through acknowledging and allowing ourselves to feel, possibly for the first time, the sorrows, the bitterness, the unfairness of it all. We've lost relationships and opportunities we can't reclaim. We must accept this and not ignore or stuff these feelings, no matter how painful. Allowing ourselves to grieve, hopefully with a friend or two by our side, is the healthy course to freedom.

This is where a community is vitally important. We need people who can empathize with us and help us process our grief in a safe manner. Our default mode is to ignore or insulate ourselves from grief, especially if we feel our behavior is the cause of it. We need to let others treat the wound so we can heal, which brings us to step four.

Forgive: This is the capstone step. Forgiveness is the absolute conclusion. Without forgiveness, the other components have no meaning. We may discover things for which we need to ask or grant forgiveness. People familiar with Alcoholics Anonymous and other 12-step programs know the importance of asking for forgiveness and making restitution whenever possible. Forgiveness releases us from bitterness and resentment. It's the path from death to life.

Each of the four steps involves letting go of old beliefs and behaviors. If we die daily to the default settings—the fallacies we've created in our heads—and adopt the mind of Christ, we can live the life Jesus offers us. He calls it abundant (John 10:10). He calls it freedom (John 8:36). It requires humility, trust, letting go, and receiving.

Just as we have a default mode for dealing with pain, we have a default mode when thinking about death: We're terrified of it. This fear causes us to ignore death as long as we can because it's so horrific to face. We try to insulate ourselves from this Brutal Reality. We are uncomfortable at funerals because we feel awkward. We don't know what to do. We don't engage in the grieving process with other people.

Here again, the mind of Christ gives us another way to understand the Brutal Reality of death. What did Jesus teach about death? "For whoever wants to save their life will lose it, but whoever loses their life for me will save it" Luke 9:24. If we try to avoid death (save our life), we will lose life. If we embrace death (lose our life), we will save it. In other words, the way to defeat death's power is to daily let go of the harmful, self-centered thoughts we've constructed. In so doing, we can say along with Paul, "I die daily." Oh, by the way, this act of letting go always feels like dying. In this regard, we're able to die before we die.

Mike Hamel: I've been close enough to the Valley of the Shadow of Death to look over the rim, but I never fell off—not that I wasn't pushed a few times. Not that I'm a stranger to death. As a pastor, I participated in many funerals, including those of my mother, father, sister, brother-in-law, niece, and numerous other family and friends.

By far, the most painful death was Susan's, my wife of thirty-seven years, who died on Thanksgiving 2011. This was all the more shocking because I was the one doing hand-to-hand combat with cancer. For three years, she'd lived in dreadful anticipation of losing me, yet I was the one left behind to grieve.

So, what happens when death's shadow crosses your path?

You're in the dark, but life goes on. At first, you just survive. Family and friends make a huge difference if you are fortunate enough to have them nearby. The passage of time helps. Your perspective changes—or it should:

People become more precious.

You get more out of everyday events.

You care less about stuff and more about experiences.

You delve more deeply into the spiritual aspects of life.

You may dodge a few bullets, but the Grim Reaper never runs out of ammo. Death gets us all in the end as surely as it picks off loved ones along the way. Until it's your turn, live in the now because yesterday never changes, and tomorrow never comes.

First, survive.

Then, live.

Then, live for and with others.

"Our bodies are finite, so there has to be a transition to the eternal," Henri Nouwen reminds us. "Part of that process is being 'mortified.' Life is a school in which we are trained to depart. That is what mortification means: training to die, to cut away the enslaving ties with the past so that what we call death is not a surprise anymore but the last of many gateways that lead to the full human person."

Jesus used another metaphor to say we should die before we die. "Unless a kernel of wheat falls to the ground and dies, it remains only a single seed. But if it dies, it produces many seeds" John 12:24. Dying is a necessary step to living. The degree to which we can embrace our mortality is the degree to which we are free to live life to the fullest. "I have come that they may have life," Jesus promised, "and that they may have it more abundantly" John 10:10 NKJV.

5

Ephraim's Story
Part 2

But a Samaritan, as he traveled, came where the man was; and when he saw him, he took pity on him. He went to him and bandaged his wounds, pouring on oil and wine. Then he put the man on his own donkey, brought him to an inn and took care of him. The next day he took out two denarii and gave them to the inn-keeper. 'Look after him,' he said, 'and when I return, I will reimburse you for any extra expense you may have.'

Luke 10:33-35

We pick up Ephraim's backstory where we left off in Chapter 3. He's coming to grips with the fact that life is hard and he will die someday. While he's grappling with these truths, two more Brutal Realities raise their gnarly heads: The world does not revolve around you, and You are not in control.

What we invent about Ephraim is rooted in real life. Hopefully, you'll see aspects of your life reflected in some of what he goes through and benefit from his example.

* * *

Ephraim had a lot to think about after his visit with Uncle Mordecai. Seeing his uncle enjoying life and hearing his story encouraged Ephraim to stick it out as a merchant. What continued to echo was, "You are a broker to your bones. Why change?" That concise phrase meant everything. The time with his uncle was a window into himself. He had gained a better understanding of his father and a new clarity and energy for the days ahead.

Ephraim went to his family's trading house in Joppa, where he found himself in a new position addressing his father. "I will continue to run the interior routes," he said, "but I will no longer assume the risks alone. The roads are too dangerous, and our losses have been unacceptable." (He didn't mention the possibility of loss of life, which was still on his mind.) You will hire guards for our shipments or find someone to take my place."

Instead of protesting, Yaakov smiled. "It's about time you grew a pair. Done."

Ephraim was pleasantly surprised. He'd expected an argument.

"A ship arrived yesterday," Yaakov said. "Select what will fetch good prices among Herod's people in

Jericho and have your brother arrange purchase. Then be on your way."

"And the guards?"

"Your brother will arrange those as well."

Two days later, Ephraim headed home with six wagons and two guards. The passage through the Ascent of Adummim on the Jericho Road wasn't as nerve-racking as before, but it gave him the chills nonetheless.

"You talked to your uncle," Johanna said when she saw her husband. "You look better."

"I feel better," Ephraim replied. He shared about his talk with Mordecai and about his father's agreement to hire guards.

With his newfound energy, Ephraim started the side business he had long dreamed about. He tried to buy dates and olives to sell along his regular routes but found the farmers had more customers than they could supply. So, he went to the markets around Herod's Winter Palace, looking for exotic goods he could buy on credit.

"Will your father guarantee the loan?" one merchant asked.

"This is my business, not my father's," Ephraim said.

"Then you will need cash until you are well established. No credit."

At the same time, Ephraim was finding out his father's concession of the guards came at a price. To cover the extra expense, Yaakov scheduled more trips without consulting Ephraim. The pace of travel left him little time to pursue his personal interests. He tried to slow things down, but his father wouldn't allow it. Instead, Yaakov took all scheduling out of Ephraim's hands and put Nathan in charge.

"I'm an employee just like the guards," Ephraim complained to Johanna on a rare day when he was home. "Nathan says "jump," and I have to ask, 'How high?' I'm in my thirties, working my butt off, and for what?"

Johanna listened intently and allowed her husband to vent his frustration.

The next time he was in Joppa, Ephraim talked to his father about the increased workload. Yaakov waved the complaint away. "More ships are coming in every month. If we don't move the cargo, someone else will."

"Do we have to move it all?" Ephraim asked. "With the extra trips, I hardly see my family."

"That's because you're in the marketplace looking for your own customers."

So, his father did know.

"That's right," Ephraim admitted. "And I'll continue to do so because our arrangement is no longer acceptable."

Yaakov remained silent.

"You and I see things differently," Ephraim said. "Do things your way, but I'm going a different way."

"Stay focused on the family business and I will see to your future," Yaakov said.

"When?" Ephraim asked.

"When I say," Yaakov shot back.

Ephraim slowly shook his head. "That no longer works, father."

Mike Hamel: In 1996, after twenty-five years in ministry, I started EMT Communications, a one-man writing and media consulting business. I had hoped writing books would be like planting an orchard. I would do the work upfront and the books would keep producing fruit I could live on while I wrote more books. But writing turned out to be more like farming. I planted a crop, harvested it, and started over the next season. It was much more hand-to-mouth, with lean times between harvests.

Even if my writing deserved attention, guess what? The publishing world didn't revolve around me. I learned this the hard way as book after book was written, published, marketed . . . and forgotten.

For example, the first two books in my *Matterhorn* series were featured in a *Focus on the Family* magazine. Focus bought 2,000 copies, and other bookstores followed suit. But after a few months, there weren't enough sales to keep my books on the shelves. Then, my publisher decided not to print the last two books in the series. Nor would they return the rights to the books until I bought back their entire inventory of more than 9,000 books. I held onto a handful as mementos; the rest were turned into pulp.

I don't do ghostwriting—writing in someone else's name—but I have put substantial editorial work into books that don't have my name on the cover. I might receive a one-sentence thank you in the Acknowledgments for six months of effort. In those cases, I settle for my name on a check, not the cover.

As of 2024, I've written or edited more than forty books. None have been even close to bestsellers. This is the experience of most full-time writers. With more than sixteen million English titles on Amazon, the likelihood of getting discovered and promoted is slim. Just because my writing is good and my stories are important doesn't mean they will be read and recommended.

I'm at peace with that. I know who I am and what I do best. It would be nice if more people knew it, but it's not necessary.

The next several months were tough, but Ephraim and Johanna managed. He found odd items to buy and sell. She made clothes and sold them in the market. One day, Mordecai came to Jericho. After a simple dinner, he said, "I see your leg is healed; let's go for a walk."

Ephraim chose a quiet, palm-lined path near the house. Mordecai spoke first. "I've been thinking about you. I could use someone with your experience in Judea. Would you be up for a joint project?"

"I would," Ephraim said. "What would it require?"

"Your full attention, for one thing. Are you ready for that?"

"I am," Ephraim replied.

"I will provide the goods," Mordecai went on. "You make the sales; we split the earnings 60—40. When can you be ready?"

"Give me two weeks to get to Joppa and back."

Yaakov wasn't happy, but Ephraim had turned a corner. In the face of uncertainty, it was time to move forward.

The arrangement turned a tidy profit, and other joint ventures followed. With Mordecai's patronage, Ephraim hired help, trained them in his business style, and expanded to more towns. There were strong headwinds. The Jews were as difficult to deal with as ever. Higher taxes cut into the profits. The olive harvest wasn't as plentiful as in years past. His father and brother did all they could to put Ephraim and Mordecai out of business. They almost succeeded, but honesty and fair treatment won out over bribes and bare-knuckle tactics.

One day, Ephraim ran into his father on the docks at Joppa. They were both eyeing the cargo of a ship from the Ivory Coast. "Stop competing with your flesh and blood," Yaakov growled.

"There's enough merchandise for both of us," Ephraim calmly replied. "I have my own business to run."

Yaakov scowled. "You have nothing but what the traitor Mordecai gives you."

"He's your brother."

"He's a traitor," Yaakov repeated.

"Because he didn't want to live in your shadow?" Ephraim fired back. "Neither do I."

"Don't deceive yourself. You are like your mother, too weak for this dog-eat-dog business."

"I used to believe that," Ephraim admitted. "It made me so angry when you wouldn't give me the chances you gave Nathan. I'm done seeing myself through your eyes. I'm done being who you think I am. Now I know better." As he turned to go, he said back over his shoulder, "Being myself is good enough."

The years passed, the business grew. When Mordecai decided to move to Rome, Ephraim bought him out. Now in his late forties, Ephraim was more at peace with himself, less prone to self-doubt and anger. He worked hard and took pride in his success but saw himself as more than a merchant.

Ephraim traveled on the Jericho Road several times a year. Whenever he climbed the Ascent of Adummim, he recalled the watershed incident that happened there. His future could've gone either way. With Mordecai's guidance, he chose to face the pain in life, accept the negative, and move forward to be who he was meant to be.

On his way home from Jerusalem one late spring day, he saw a man in the ditch not far from where he'd had his accident years ago. The figure was bloody and motionless. Ephraim wasn't sure the man was alive until one of his hands moved slightly, as if reaching for help. Ephraim went to him and began gently cleaning his wounds. When he regained consciousness, Ephraim put the man on his donkey, brought him to an inn, and cared for him. The next day he took out two *denarii* and gave them to the innkeeper. "Look after him," he said, "and when I return, I will reimburse you for any extra expense you may have."

Mike Haddorff: We don't often think about the robbery victim, but if we imagine a backstory for him as we've done for the other characters in this story, he had a past and a future—if someone would give him another chance. I'm all for second, third, etc., chances.

I started and ran my own electrical business for more than 40 years. During that time, I interviewed many people for jobs in the field and the office. Occasionally, I would have someone begin a job interview with the words, "I need to tell you something about me." The first time it happened, I was in my 30s. A man not much younger than me was applying for a journeyman position.

What came after the phrase "I need to tell you something about me" was that he'd been incarcerated for a serious felony. While in prison, he studied the electrical trade and worked as an electrician. He had his state license and all the experience necessary. He'd been released and needed a job. I needed help, but I was fearful about his past. I couldn't bring myself to trust him in his rehabilitation process. It was too much for me to bite off, so I didn't hire him.

Fast-forward a few decades, and I'm in my mid-fifties. A young man applied for an apprenticeship I had open. He'd also been convicted of a serious crime and had served time. While incarcerated, he learned the solar trade and earned some certifications. He was interested in solar, and we were doing solar projects. I had changed enough by now that I hired the guy. Over time, he did very well. Today, he has his own business and is doing great.

What changed me was life experience. I had made some good decisions and some horrible decisions. I survived near bankruptcy. I suffered the ins and outs of everyday life, from boredom to absolute terror. Because of all this, I listened to this young man differently. He just wanted another chance, and I wanted to give it to him.

In this case, it turned out marvelously. That doesn't always happen, but regardless of the outcome, it's a good idea to give people another chance.

6

Brutal Realities Three and Four

Brutal Realities One and Two have to do with *pain*: Life is hard, and you are going to die. Engaging with them involves learning how to face and process pain and mortality in a healthy way. Brutal Realities Three and Four have to do with *power:* The world does not revolve around you, and you are not in control. Engaging with them involves learning you aren't who you think you need to be and that freedom and joy come from letting go rather than clamping down.

In Chapter 5, Ephraim constantly ran up against his lack of power. He stood up to his father but found he was still under Dad's thumb. His efforts at self-employment met with little success. But he persevered and, with Mordecai's help, discovered that being himself—not who others thought he was—was enough. He faced his fear, recognized opportunities as they came his way, and pursued what would make him a healthier, more compassionate man.

Ephraim's story illustrates how wrestling with the Brutal Realities helps us find our place in the world. Maturity comes when we grasp who we really are and where the power for abundant living comes from.

* * *

When we say, "The world does not revolve around you," who is the "you"? Our sense of who we are comes from our identity. This is shaped over our lifetime by several factors or voices speaking to us. These include our personality (self-talk), culture (social feedback), experience (direct knowledge), education (worldview), and life context (immediate surroundings). The volume at which they speak varies from time to time. The voices combine to tell us who we think we are, which becomes our default self-image. We're aware of some of this, but much of it we aren't, and that's normal.

For many folks, the feedback is generally positive, and they have a fairly healthy self-image. For others, unfortunately, the message is that we are less than what we should be. We don't measure up when compared to others. You went to college; she got her MBA from Harvard. You drive a Ford; he owns two BMWs. You work in the bullpen; he has a corner office.

We think we're not good enough from birth; we believe our behavior is what defines us. (We dealt with

72

this misunderstanding in our book, *Birth, Not Behavior*.) Therefore, we're compelled to do things to create and maintain a good self-image in our heads and in the eyes of others. Our accomplishments become the measure of our self-worth.

Propping up our self-image isn't a one-time effort; it's more like keeping a hot-air balloon aloft, and the bigger the better. Hundreds of books have been written about the importance of positive self-talk. From the outside, we need constant feedback and validation, the *oohs* and *aahs* of others. We want to know how we're doing, and no matter how well, it's never good enough. There's always another hurdle.

But there's another way to see ourselves, and that's with the mind of Christ. It starts with realizing we are "God's handiwork (*poema*), created in Christ Jesus to do good works, which God prepared in advance for us to do" (Ephesians 2:10). We are God's poem, his work of art. The Greek word *poema* means "that which is made." There are no duplicates; each poem is unique and priceless! He not only created us with a purpose; he sustains us moment by moment.

Jesus had a clear sense of purpose and an awareness of a moment-by-moment connection with his father. He knew he was loved and operated out of this knowledge. He invites us to think and do the same. "As the Father has loved me, so have I loved you. Now remain in my love. If you keep my commands, you will remain in my love, just as I have kept my Father's commands and remain in his love. I have told you this so that *my joy* may be in you and that *your joy* may be complete" (John 15:9-11).

When we see ourselves as God's children, unconditionally loved and created with a purpose, we are sharing the mind of Christ. We can live daily as he did. Regardless of what shape our life has taken so far, we can embrace what is true about us today. The challenge for most of us lies in believing this truth instead of accepting our default identity, which says we aren't enough and must earn God's love and the respect of others through our behavior. We have a moment-by-moment choice to believe this lie or to embrace God's truth about us. When we believe him, we move from "I am less" thinking to "I am loved" thinking. This is the mind of Christ.

If I'm in the center of creating my own identity, then my world revolves around me. My thinking and actions are about me building a better me. When I let go of this notion and embrace who God says I am, then I can assume the role and play the part God has designed me for. This is way less exhausting.

Mike Haddorff: I owned and operated a small business from 1980-2020. I made a lot of mistakes, but sometimes,

I did a pretty good job. What's hard about owning your own business is that you must keep showing up, day after day, month after month, year after year, doing the same thing over and over. This has a way of wearing you down.

Being someone who aims to please takes a lot of work to maintain over the years. There's an upside regarding customer support but also a downside. I was easily manipulated into believing that whatever the issue was, it was my fault.

At one time, I worked with a fellow who was good at what he did but was a bit short on enthusiasm for life. Because of my need to fix things, which I was unaware of at the time, I believed his bland-to-sour response was my problem. I thought if I did my job correctly, he would wake up and smell the roses.

Every morning I'd arrive at work wondering how full his glass would be. On good days, I would drive home happy; life was good. On sour days, I left wondering *what's wrong with me.* What's ironic about this whole thing is I was sucked in and didn't realize it.

One day, I woke up to this craziness. I can't say I was angry. It was more about the fact that *I didn't want to do this anymore.* I was able to zoom out and watch myself from a different perspective. As I did, I thought, *This is crazy. This is helping no one, especially me.*

That morning, after settling in, I stepped into his office. "Can we talk?" We went into my office and sat at the conference table. "I don't know the details of what you're going through," I said, "but working with you is very difficult. I know you're not happy, and I feel bad about that, but from now on, I want you to know I'm not going to bend my world to try and make you happy. That's over as of today. I want a good relationship with you, but I no longer believe your moods are my fault."

Two weeks later, he quit.

The fourth Brutal Reality is that you are not in control. When I (Mike Haddorff) teach this, I use a box to illustrate life. We can experience many wonderful things and enjoy quality relationships in this box. But as we enjoy life in the box, there's also a pull to move to something outside we perceive as greater but unfamiliar. This longing can be called transcendence. Feeling it is part of being human. I call this The Greater Pull. Because God is behind it, it's always a pull, never a push. It draws us to go beyond ourselves and our environment.

When opportunities arise to go outside the box, however, we don't often take them because this requires going over what I call the threshold of fear (T.O.F.). It's the fear of moving into unknown territory, and it scares the heck out of us, so we clamp down, which bounces us back from the doorway in response to fear. It's the fear of moving into unknown territory that is actually the fear of losing self-created and defined power. This fear of losing control (power) causes us to stay rooted in the reality we know instead of crossing over into unfamiliar territory.

We clamp because it's our default mode to maintain personal power. We then rationalize our clamping because we need some sort of explanation to avoid feeling bad about ourselves. Rationalizing is our way of telling a story we can live with, a story where we're comfortable and in control. But this is just smoke and mirrors. When we clamp down because of fear, we get into a cycle that keeps us inside our box. Round and round we go. Eventually, this cycle becomes our life. We resist the Greater Pull to grow and settle for a smaller box where we have the illusion of control.

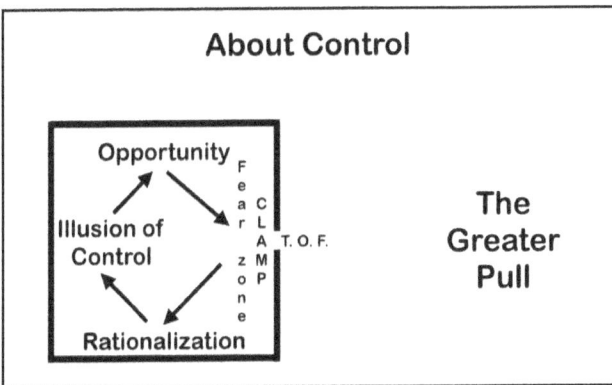

About Control

Opportunity

Illusion of Control

Rationalization

Fear Zone

C L A M P   T. O. F.

The Greater Pull

Think of your hand as another metaphor. It can be clenched into a fist with the fingers digging into the palm, or it can be open to shake a stranger's hand, grab a rope to rappel down a wall, pick up a seashell while snorkeling, or whatever. So, how do we go from a closed fist to an open hand?

There's an alternative to clamping down in fear. When we decide to move outside the box, it can feel like falling because we let go of being in control. Moving beyond the fear zone takes trust. It requires seeing life with the mind of Christ, in other words, the way Jesus saw it. He trusted his father was in control, so he didn't have to be. He could let go, trusting he was safe. "Who, being in very nature God, did not consider equality with God something to be used to his own advantage ('grasped' in the American Standard Version); rather, he made himself nothing by taking the very nature of a servant, being made in human likeness" (Philippians 2:6-7).

Jesus demonstrated that true strength lies in letting go, a lesson Paul repeated in 2 Corinthians 12:10: "For when I am weak, then I am strong." This weakness Paul described is a letting go of one's agenda and a leaning into the truth of who God says we are. This is where trust comes in. We can get past the threshold of fear and through the door to greater opportunities by leaning into the truth of how God thinks about us.

```
┌─────────────────────────────────────────────────┐
│      How To Move Outside The Box                 │
│                                                  │
│    ┌──────────────────────┐                      │
│    │  Opportunity  F       │                     │
│    │        ↗↘    e  C      │        The          │
│    │            a  L       │                     │
│    │  Illusion of  r A·····►Trust   Greater      │
│    │  Control    z M       │        Pull         │
│    │        ↖      o P      │                     │
│    │         ↘    n        │                     │
│    │            e          │                     │
│    │  Rationalization      │                     │
│    └──────────────────────┘                      │
└─────────────────────────────────────────────────┘
```

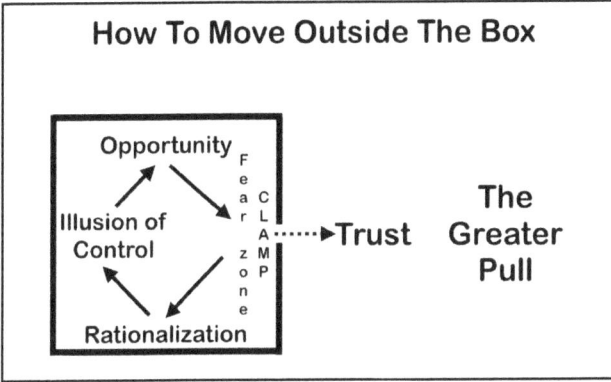

Once we follow the Greater Pull outside, our lives expand into a bigger box, a process that can be repeated over and over. Each time we let go of needing to be in control and overcome the fear of the unknown by trusting in God, not ourselves, we experience the more abundant life Jesus promised.

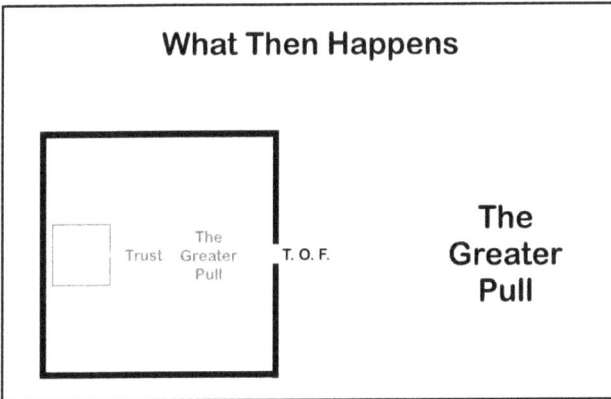

```
┌─────────────────────────────────────────────────┐
│              What Then Happens                   │
│                                                  │
│   ┌──────────────────────────┐                   │
│   │                          │      The          │
│   │ ┌────┐    The            │     Greater       │
│   │ │    │ Trust Greater T.O.F.│    Pull         │
│   │ └────┘    Pull           │                   │
│   │                          │                   │
│   └──────────────────────────┘                   │
└─────────────────────────────────────────────────┘
```

A poem by Rainer Rilke called *The Man Watching* beautifully captures the idea of being overcome

by what is greater than ourselves as the path to true
strength. It reads in part:

> What we choose to fight is so tiny!
> What fights with us is so great.
> If only we would let ourselves be dominated
> as things do by some immense storm,
> we would become strong too, and not need names.
>
> When we win it's with small things,
> and the triumph itself makes us small.
> What is extraordinary and eternal
> does not want to be bent by us.
> I mean the Angel who appeared
> to the wrestlers of the Old Testament:
> when the wrestlers' sinews
> grew long like metal strings,
> he felt them under his fingers
> like chords of deep music.
>
> Whoever was beaten by this Angel
> (who often simply declined the fight)
> went away proud and strengthened
> and great from that harsh hand,
> that kneaded him as if to change his shape.
> Winning does not tempt that man.
> This is how he grows: by being defeated, decisively,
> by constantly greater beings.

We grow by "being defeated, decisively, by constantly greater beings." We move outside the small box of our current circumstances by allowing ourselves to be overcome because we trust in a strength beyond ourselves. We live as though when we are weak, we are strong, the same way Jesus lived.

When it comes to Brutal Realities Three and Four concerning power, we must wake up to what is actually true. We are not inadequate; we are God's work of art and unconditionally loved as his children. We do not control our lives by clamping down; we are the most alive when we allow ourselves to be overcome.

Mike Hamel: I became a Christian through the outreach of a house church affiliated with the Plymouth Brethren, a conservative, nondenominational denomination. I spent the next twenty-five years with them. The time was full of positive experiences and loving people, but also several brushes with the Brutal Reality that I was not in control. Many of the situations I found myself in with the Brethren were beyond my ability to change or accept.

One area that rubbed me wrong was the role of women. The PBs held to a literal view of 1 Timothy 2:12, "I do not permit a woman to teach or to assume authority over a man; she must be quiet." Women couldn't be elders or deacons, teach from the platform, or speak in worship meetings. They could sing and teach children in Sunday school, albeit under the authority of the male elders.

I couldn't sway the leadership at my local church to take a more egalitarian view. I could stay and enjoy the fellowship in this restricted environment or look for somewhere with a broader view. I chose the latter and moved to Chicago to become the Director of the Resource Center at Interest Ministries in 1990.

Interest was a service organization on the progressive end of a conservative movement. Conservates didn't like us serving churches that didn't do things in the biblical (read: Plymouth Brethren) way. To stop us, they filed a lawsuit to cut off our funding from a major foundation. Never mind that the Bible says not to take your brothers to court, 1 Corinthians 6:1-8.

Yet again, I found myself in a situation I could neither control nor change. By this time, I'd had enough of passionate believers fighting over petty issues. I was done with the Holy Huddle. I resigned from Interest, moved back to Colorado Springs, and hung out my shingle as a writer.

Several times along my life path, I left behind good salaries and great co-workers to pursue opportunities for growth. There was always a cost, but it was a price I was willing to pay.

The Serenity Prayer asks, "God, grant me the serenity to accept the things I cannot change, the courage to change the things I can, and the wisdom to know the difference." God granted me the wisdom to accept that I couldn't change an almost 200-year-old sect. He gave me the courage to change what I could—my participation—and serenity to accept how life has turned out.

7

What Happened
Next . . .

"Which of these three do you think was a neighbor to the man who fell into the hands of robbers?"

The expert in the law replied, "The one who had mercy on him."

Jesus told him, "Go and do likewise."

Luke 10:36-37

While the story of the Good Samaritan is fictional, the expert in the law—a man we call Simeon—was a real person with a serious question he'd spent much of his life studying: "What must I do to inherit eternal life?" It's a question many religions seek to answer. Jesus' answer focused on the here and now: Help those in need.

It's not enough that Simeon agreed he should love his neighbor; he must follow the Samaritan's example. What we portray happening to Simeon happened to many people who encountered Jesus; they were radically changed.

* * *

Jesus' simple story answered Simeon's question on how to inherit eternal life. It bypassed the debates about the finer points of the law Simeon was used to and went to the heart of the matter, albeit in an unexpected way. When Simeon admitted the Samaritan had done the right thing, Jesus looked into his eyes and said, "Go and do likewise."

This direct statement caught Simeon off guard. It wasn't as easy as Jesus made it out to be. But before he could argue the point, Jesus moved on.

On the walk back to Jerusalem, Simeon mulled over the parable. As a Levite himself and someone who served in the Temple, he could understand why the priest and the Levite had not helped the robbery victim. They hid behind the letter of the law regarding ritual purity to ignore the clear command to show mercy to those in need.

But should mercy be extended to everyone, no matter the circumstances? What about holiness?

Then there was the Samaritan, a heretic who did what the prophet Micah said pleased God: "And what does the Lord require of you? To act justly and to love mercy and to walk humbly with your God." But God also required his people to walk in holiness. That's why his law specified everything from what to eat to how to dress to when to pray.

In the following days, Simeon couldn't get the parable out of his mind. He thought of more precise questions and wondered if he could get a private audience with Jesus as his friend Nicodemus had. The next best thing would be to talk to Nicodemus. Meanwhile, he set out to learn everything he could about Jesus.

When Nicodemus returned to Jerusalem the following month, Simeon invited him over for Sabbath. He told Nicodemus about questioning Jesus and repeated the story of the Samaritan.

Nicodemus smiled as he listened. "This itinerant preacher gets to the heart of things more quickly than those of us who have spent our whole lives studying the law."

"But he interprets God's law as if he's above it," Simeon said. "My students report just such claims. Jesus once told a crowd of hundreds, 'You have heard it said, you shall not murder, and anyone who murders will be subject to judgment. But I tell you that anyone who is angry with a brother or sister will be subject to judgment.'"

Nicodemus started to speak, but Simeon kept going. "Jesus also told the people, 'You have heard it said, love your neighbor and hate your enemy. But I tell you, love your enemies and pray for those who persecute you.'"

"He goes beyond the law," Nicodemus agreed, "but does he go counter to it?"

"Yes," Simeon replied. "And not just in his teaching. He eats with tax collectors and harlots. He consorts with unclean Samaritans and Romans. He violates the very Sabbath we are observing."

"And yet, his words and actions stir up the people like the prophets of old," Nicodemus pointed out. "He has stirred our hearts, or we wouldn't be having this conversation."

"But is he a false prophet?"

Nicodemus shrugged. "Time will tell."

Mike Hamel: Christians are people who have a relationship with Jesus Christ. They are either baptized into his church at birth or born again into it as adults. I've experienced both, and my concept of Jesus has changed along the way.

As a Catholic, I grew up seeing Jesus as a bloody, emaciated man on a crucifix. He was not nearly as appealing as his kindly mother. As a born-again Protestant, I saw posters of the Che Guevara-like Jesus of the Jesus revolution. As an evangelical pastor, I saw Jesus portrayed as the champion of social causes and political candidates. On the TV series The Chosen, I saw an approachable Jesus I'd love to hang out with.

Most people have some concept of Jesus because, as historian Paul Johnson wrote, "Jesus of Nazareth was, in terms of influence, the most important human being in history. He is also the most written about and discussed." All this impact from a small trove of source documents: a few epistles written within twenty or thirty years of his death, four biographies penned within fifty to seventy years, and fewer than fifty corroborating documents in circulation by 100 CE.

One reason for his unprecedented popularity through the ages is his malleability. By that, I mean the ability of people to shape Jesus into a Christ of their choosing. How do we separate historical fact from subjective interpretation? With great difficulty and a lot of guesswork.

For several years, I've worked at unlearning what I'd been taught about Jesus, stripping away the veneers added over the centuries. At times, the Catholic Jesus, Protestant Jesus, Evangelical Jesus, Republican Jesus, or Mike Hamel Jesus seem a far cry from the biblical Jesus. By questioning these interpretations, I'm making space for the living Christ to appear. He's the Word beyond the words we use to describe him. He's the mystery beyond the metaphors like son, shepherd, king, and Christ. He's immanent and transcendent, approachable and unknowable.

False prophet or true? This was the question Simeon devoted himself to answering. He paid close attention to the stories about Jesus and tried to sift fact from fiction—a difficult task because Jesus was a walking, talking contradiction. He had said, "Not one jot or one tittle from the law shall pass away until everything is accomplished." And yet he ignored the purification and dietary laws and encouraged others to do likewise.

Then there were the miracles. Jesus reportedly cast out demons, healed the sick, and restored sight to the blind. Simeon himself had talked to a man born blind who had received his sight at Jesus' hands. Simeon had gone so far as to interview the man's parents to ensure this wasn't a sham.

It wasn't.

A priest at the Temple told Simeon of a man claiming to be a leper who said Jesus had healed him and told him to present the prescribed sacrifice for cleansing. On the other hand, Jesus challenged the very Temple where he'd sent the leper. He criticized the teachers of the law and the priests who served there, at one point calling some of them a brood of vipers.

And then there were rumors that couldn't possibly be true: Jesus walking on water and feeding more than 5,000 people with a few loaves and fishes. Preposterous! Yet Simeon couldn't dismiss *all* the astonishing words and deeds attributed to Jesus nor deny the power of his radical love.

As Simeon's mind wrestled with the enigma that was the Galilean, his heart resonated with the message Jesus powerfully preached and lived. It could be summed up in the words of the great rabbi Hillel, "Love God, love your neighbor; the rest is commentary."

Mike Haddorff: I was a guest at a men's campfire discussion and the leader asked me where I was in my spiritual journey and how I'd gotten there. I said my early years were about *joining up* to the faith. I was big on the soldier metaphor, "Go get 'em for Jesus." My middle years were about **straightening up** in my faith, meaning "white knuckling effort to find the golden key to this thing called spirituality." It has taken me well into my sixties to let go of this notion and realize it is about **waking up** to what's already true.

The guys wanted details. "Just tell us what to do."

I couldn't give them a list of dos and don'ts. But I did give them a focal point, a place to fix their attention as they moved forward: Jesus. I shared that I've been a lifelong student and teacher of the Bible. Along the way, I've become more and more enamored with Jesus.

I started as a conservative evangelical concerned about pleasing God. Now, I'm interested in following Jesus. *How did Jesus think?* I ask myself. I examine him in the Gospels, the epistles, and the Old Testament, but I'm also more aware of him beyond the pages of Scripture. After all, "in him we live and move and have our being," as Paul says.

I used to be like the young fish in a scene from the Pixar movie Soul:

I heard this story about a fish, he swims up to an older fish and says: "I'm trying to find this thing they call the ocean." "The ocean?" the older fish says, "that's what you're in right now." "This," says the young fish, "this is water. What I want is the ocean!"

Waking up to being in Christ moment by moment is my joy heading into my seventies.

It was a beautiful autumn day, and Jerusalem was brimful of pilgrims who came to celebrate *Sukkot*, the feast of Tabernacles. It was one of the three feasts for which the Torah commanded all Jews to come to the Temple.

Simeon and other members of the Great Sanhedrin had just come from the Courtyard of the Gentiles. He had never liked how that sacred space was crammed with animals and money changers, but there was nothing he could do about it. Pilgrims had to change their Roman money for currency without graven images to pay the Temple tax or buy approved sacrifices. The money changers set the exchange rate, which was outrageous.

What Happened Next . . .

Simeon didn't know which he detested more, priest-sanctioned extortion or that it was carried on in the Temple. He noted the avarice in the priests' eyes as they mentally tallied the profits they would soon be enjoying. A few members of the Sanhedrin with family ties to the priests shared their delight. They knew the Romans would stay out of the way for their cut in the lucrative business of being God's middlemen.

Amid the crowds on the Temple steps, a space began to spread like a crack in a stone wall. The source of the split soon became visible in the gap. A leper, obviously in the final stages of the dreaded disease, was slowly moving up the stairs.

No one dared touch him. No pilgrim who had traveled so far or spent so much to fulfill their religious duty was about to become unclean at the last minute for someone who had no right to be there.

"That's disgusting," said the man next to Simeon. Nathaniel was the *Av Beit Din*, the second highest-ranking member of the Sanhedrin. "If he dies there, it will make the steps unclean and hinder the flow of worshippers. We can't allow that." He called a guard and pointed to the leper. "Remove that abomination quickly."

"What should I do with him?" the guard asked.

"I don't care. Just get him out of here."

As the guard moved to obey, Simeon reached out his arm to stop him. "Perhaps the man only wants to fulfill his duty in the Temple before he dies," he said.

"According to the law, his duty is to come nowhere near this holy place," Nathaniel said. "You, of all people, should know that."

"God looks beyond the body to the heart," Simeon replied. "Shouldn't we?" He handed the scroll he'd been holding to Nathaniel. He removed his cloak, gave it to the guard, and started toward the leper.

"Let the guard do that," Nathaniel called after him. "You will be unclean."

Simeon kept walking.

"Come back here!" Nathaniel shouted.

The outcry drew attention to Simeon. Heads turned to follow him as he made his way to the leper. A wave of murmurs swelled and then stilled as Simeon greeted the man and used his sleeve to wipe the leper's sweaty brow.

The leper cringed in fear at this attention—until his eyes met Simeon's. The compassion he saw there brought tears to his own eyes. He listened to Simeon's comforting words, a sound he had not heard in years. He feebly reached out a four-fingered hand and touched Simeon's cheek in gratitude.

Simeon smiled. He carefully placed the man's spindly arm around his shoulder and helped him toward the Temple, not away from it.

"STOP HIM!" Nathaniel screamed.

The guards hurried to obey but slowed as they neared the odd pair. Something about Simeon's calmness and compassion paralyzed them with wonder. He wasn't carrying out his religious duty to keep the Temple holy. He was gently supporting the leper the way a mother would a crippled child.

With tears streaming down his face, the leper kept murmuring, "Thank you, thank you, thank you," as they climbed the stairs. Near the top, he straightened, looked at Simeon, and asked, "Why help me?"

"Because as one of God's children, you are welcome in his house."

Simeon thought for a moment, then added. "And because you are my neighbor."

Clean and Unclean

Jesus put two religious people in his parable of the Good Samaritan: the priest and the Levite. One possible reason they refused to help someone in need was because they thought the contact would defile their relationship with God. This way of thinking and acting reflects a human archetype regarding clean and unclean.

The psychologist Carl Jung defined archetypes as "reoccurring patterns or symbols existing universally and instinctively in the collective unconscious of man." One archetype we share is the distinction between clean and unclean. The difference is natural and important. Clean is healthy; unclean is unhealthy. Healthy behaviors promote life; unhealthy behaviors promote death.

We can use an archery metaphor to illustrate this idea. Aiming for and hitting the bullseye is important because the bullseye represents life. The outlying circles or missing the target altogether are various levels of death because they are misaligned with life.

Another name for the bullseye is clean; everything else is various degrees of unclean. Some attitudes and behaviors are life-giving, clean, healthy, good, and holy, and some attitudes and behaviors are deadly, unclean, unhealthy, evil, and unholy. The more we hit the bullseye, the more we enjoy life. The farther we are from healthy habits and relationships, the more likely we are to experience ill health and early death.

This metaphor applies to morality as well. Clean behaviors promote life and joy for ourselves and others, while unclean behaviors promote ill health and pain for ourselves and others.

This otherwise healthy way of thinking goes awry when we think God is happy with us when our behavior hits the bullseye and unhappy when we miss. Because he is perfect, we assume he requires perfection. We see him as a strict disciplinarian and the Bible as his rulebook. True, God our Father wants us to aim for the bullseye, but it's because, like any good parent, he loves his children and wants to keep us safe and healthy. He wants the best for us but doesn't require the best from us to earn his love. His love is our birthright.

Many religions encourage the perception that God is pleased when we hit the mark and upset when we miss. The Greek word for sin, 'hamartia,' means to miss the mark. Religious marks are so detailed that pleasing

God by hitting them is almost impossible. The constant stress of not measuring up keeps us from trusting in his unconditional love.

The Judeo-Christian worldview is based on the Bible, which has much to say about clean and unclean. The Law of Moses goes into minute detail about relationships, food, clothes, work, and many other facets of life that are divided into clean and unclean. This distinction served two purposes: First, to establish a standard of behavior "so that you can distinguish between the holy and the common, between the unclean and the clean" (Leviticus 10:10). Second, to set the Jews apart from other nations, "Observe them carefully, for this will show your wisdom and understanding to the nations, who will hear about all these decrees and say, 'Surely this great nation is a wise and understanding people'" (Deuteronomy 4:6).

Think of the words *holy* and *separate*: Holy to God and separate from others.

Being holy and separate is good when properly understood. However, over time, general principles like clean and unclean got overgrown by human re-definitions that went counter to the original intent. One name for this is legalism. Merriam-Webster defines it as "strict, literal, or excessive conformity to the law or a religious or moral code." Legalism is a distortion of a valid distinction.

In the centuries between Moses and Jesus, the Jews in general and the Pharisees in particular adopted a legalistic mindset. They became so focused on being holy and separate that they lost sight of the weightier matters of the law. "Woe to you, teachers of the law and Pharisees (literally, 'separated ones')," Jesus scolded. "You hypocrites! You give a tenth of your spices—mint, dill, and cumin. But you have neglected the more important matters of the law—justice, mercy and faithfulness" (Matthew 23:23). Another time, he addressed the dietary laws the Jews scrupulously followed. "What goes into someone's mouth does not defile them, but what comes out of their mouth, that is what defiles them" (Matthew 15:11). And when he disregarded some of the Sabbath laws, he insisted "The Sabbath was made for man, not man for the Sabbath" (Mark 2:27).

Jesus hinted at this legalism in his parable of the Good Samaritan. His audience would assume the priest and Levite didn't help the robbery victim because the law required them to stay clean to perform their religious duties. They thought remaining clean took precedence over helping someone in dire need. Jesus showed that loving your neighbor meant caring for those in need, even if they were unclean. Compassion and mercy must win out over legalism because they reflect who God is.

"Compassion isn't just about feeling the pain of others," says Father Gregory Boyle, founder of Homeboy

Industries, the largest gang intervention program in the world, "it's about bringing them in toward yourself. If we love what God loves, then, in compassion, margins get erased. 'Be compassionate as God is compassionate' means the dismantling of barriers that exclude."

Legalism leads to spiritual pride and the conviction that God favors us more than those who don't adhere to our enlightened view. We take pride in our cleanness while looking down on the unholy the way the Jews did on Samaritans and the priest and Levite did on the man in the ditch. We evade the opportunity and obligation to help others because we think they are unclean in God's eyes. Today that might be because they are non-Christian, atheists, of a different ethnic origin, transgender, gay, immigrant, or whatever group deserves God's displeasure. Our reasoning goes something like this: *They brought suffering on themselves by their sinful behavior. God is judging them for their wickedness. To do anything to lessen their suffering would be going against God.*

Humans are tribal by nature. We think our tribe is clean because this is what we've been taught. Growing up Catholic, I (Mike Hamel) was taught the priest could forgive my sin and that I received grace by swallowing the literal Body of Christ in communion. It made me clean. What made me unclean was missing Mass on Sunday, not obeying the priest, or not giving up certain things for Lent. I thought God required these practices and was pleased when I observed them. When I didn't, I was unclean and had to go to confession and do penance to receive forgiveness.

On the Protestant side, I (Mike Haddorff) cut my teeth as an impressionable young man on the idea our little group of Christians had God's truth. The groupthink was that other nice people were out there, but if they were really with it, they would meet in God's appointed way, as we did every Sunday. "We" were clean, and "they" were unclean. I swallowed this hook, line, and sinker, no questions asked. Legalism leads to spiritual pride and the conviction that God favors us more than those who don't adhere to our enlightened view.

Love draws people together in compassion, which means "to suffer together." Legalism separates people into "us" and "them." If only we could see all God's children the way he does. "There is no 'them' and 'us,'" as Gregory Boyle says. "There is only 'us.'"

* * *

Points to ponder:

- Clean and unclean are helpful distinctions. Clean is healthy, and unclean is unhealthy. Healthy behaviors promote life, and unhealthy behaviors promote death.
- The Bible has rules, but it's not a rulebook. Its laws and rules promote health and life. Some are

absolute and timeless; others are culturally bound and temporary.

- Many rules reflect the culture that instituted them, not the character of God. It's always good to ask, "How should I think about this now?"
- Principles are more important than practices. When there's an apparent clash, honor the principle, even if it breaks a rule.
- Obedience has rewards, and disobedience has penalties, but keeping the rules isn't the basis of our relationship with God. He loves us unconditionally because we are his children.
- Loving our neighbors means treating them with mercy and compassion, to suffer with, not separate from. We should treat others as family, not enemies.
- Love unites; legalism divides. Look for what we have in common, not for what divides us.

At this place within the journey, I (Mike Haddorff) am quite aware of the magnitude of help I've received to move forward in our joint endeavors at Christ in the Rockies. As in our first book, I'd like to thank these individuals in three broad groups:

The founding board members who believed in me and the idea of Christ in the Rockies. And for those who served on the board over the years, many for more than one term. I'm forever grateful for your support.

Early financial supporters who shared the cost of creating an entity, designing a website, buying insurance, and other miscellaneous expenses of incorporating and starting a nonprofit ministry. And to our financial donors who have invested in the vision year after year.

The scores and scores of volunteers who have helped with the nuts and bolts and heavy lifting of setting up and taking down several camps each year—over and over and over again.

I do want to mention by name the individuals who made this book possible: Tim Strickland, Rob Strouse, Tim FitzGerald, Matt McConnell, and David Saylor.

Recommended Reading

Boyle, Gregory. *Tattoos on the Heart: The Power of Boundless Compassion.* (Los Angeles, CA: Free Press, 2010).

Boyle, Gregory. *The Whole Language: The Power of Extravagant Tenderness,* (New York: Avid Reader Press / Simon & Schuster, 2023).

Enns, Peter. *How the Bible Actually Works: In Which I Explain How An Ancient, Ambiguous, and Diverse Book Leads Us to Wisdom Rather Than Answers—and Why That's Great News* (San Francisco, CA: HarperOne, 2019).

Frankl, Victor. *Man's Search for Meaning.* (Boston, MA: Beacon Press, 1959).

Rohr, Richard. Adam's Return: *The Five Promises of Male Spirituality.* (Redwood City, CA: PublishDrive, 2004).

Yancey, Philip. *Where the Light Fell: A Memoir.* (London: Hodder & Stoughton, 2021).

Chapter 1 | Simeon's Question

Group Discussion

1. Jesus often taught in parables. His fictional stories told the truth. Does something have to be factual to be truthful? Explain.

2. What do you think motivated Simeon to ask his question?

3. How would you answer Simeon's question, "What must I do to inherit eternal life?" How is your answer different from the one Jesus gave?

Going Inward

When it comes to your faith, are you more conservative or curious? Are you comfortable where you are, or would you like to shift more in one direction or the other? Set a timer for ten minutes and start writing about this question until time is up. For your eyes only, don't worry about what comes out; just get your initial thoughts down.

Chapter 2 | Jesus' Answer

Group Discussion

1. Why didn't the priest or Levite help the robbery victim?

2. Who are those you find yourself moving to the other side of the road to avoid? Why?

3. The Samaritans were religious, but the Jews saw them as heretics and shunned them. Given your religious background, who are the people you shun as heretics? What makes them heretics?

Going Inward

Has there been a time when you have been helped by a stranger who had no expectation of repayment? How did the experience change you? Set a timer for ten minutes and start writing about this question until time is up. For your eyes only, don't worry about what comes out; just get your initial thoughts down.

Chapter 3 | Ephraim's Story, Part 1

Group Discussion

1. What kind of pain is Ephraim experiencing?

2. What obstacles have you encountered in your career or home life that have stopped you from growing? Is there anything you can do about them?

3. Have you had an experience where you came face to face with your mortality? If so, what was it, and how did it change you?

Going Inward

In what ways in your life right now can you identify with Ephraim in his pain? Set a timer for ten minutes and start writing about this question until time is up. For your eyes only, don't worry about what comes out; just get your initial thoughts down.

Chapter 4 | Brutal Realities One and Two

Group Discussion

1. How was pain processed in your home?

2. All of us have experienced some level of wounding as children. What are some ways children deal with it?

3. To include the negative means accepting something we'd rather not face as being true. What does that mean to you?

Going Inward

Can you identify a box you would like to bring out of the basement? Set a timer for ten minutes and start writing about this question until time is up. For your eyes only, don't worry about what comes out; just get your initial thoughts down.

Chapter 5 | Ephraim's Story, part 2

Group Discussion

1. How did Ephraim's self-image change, and what led to those changes?

2. How did Ephraim's change affect his relationship with his father?

3. How did your upbringing and education prepare you to deal with setbacks in your life and career? What was helpful? What was lacking?

Going Inward

How do you perceive yourself, and how are other voices shaping who you think you need to be?

Set a timer for ten minutes and start writing about this question until time is up. For your eyes only, don't worry about what comes out; just get your initial thoughts down.

Chapter 6 | Brutal Realities Three and Four

Group Discussion

1. Which of the voices shaping your self-identity has been the most influential in your life? Why?

2. Why is it so hard to move from "I am less" thinking to "I am loved" thinking?

3. What does it mean that when we are weak, we are strong? How did Jesus model this approach to life?

Going Inward

Personal growth occurs as we allow ourselves to be conquered by ever-greater forces (reread Rilke's poem on page 80). What does this idea mean to you? What questions does it raise? What hope does it provide? Set a timer for ten minutes and start writing about this question until time is up. For your eyes only, don't worry about what comes out; just get your initial thoughts down.

Chapter 7 | What Happened Next ...

Group Discussion

1. Have you ever gone out of your way to help someone who was "unclean," as Simeon did in the Temple? What were the circumstances, and what happened as a result?

2. Should mercy and compassion be extended to everyone, even if their dire circumstances are their fault?

3. What are some things that keep us from helping people in need?

Going Inward

Ephraim was a Good Samaritan in his context (a merchant on the Jericho Road). Simeon became a good Samaritan in his context (a Levite in the temple). In what contexts might you become a Good Samaritan? Set a timer for ten minutes and start writing about this question until time is up. For your eyes only, don't worry about what comes out; just get your initial thoughts down.

Afterword

Group Discussion

1. Why did God distinguish between clean and unclean in the laws he gave his people?

2. What are some things you were taught were unclean that you now see differently? What changed your mind?

3. What are some situations where you might disobey a religious law to keep a principle, e.g., Jesus healing on the Sabbath or eating with sinners?

Going Inward

Jesus talked about "eternal life" in the here and now when he said, "go and do likewise," as demonstrated by the Good Samaritan. How does this affect your view of eternal life? Set a timer for ten minutes and start writing about this question until time is up. For your eyes only, don't worry about what comes out; just get your initial thoughts down.

More Questions Online

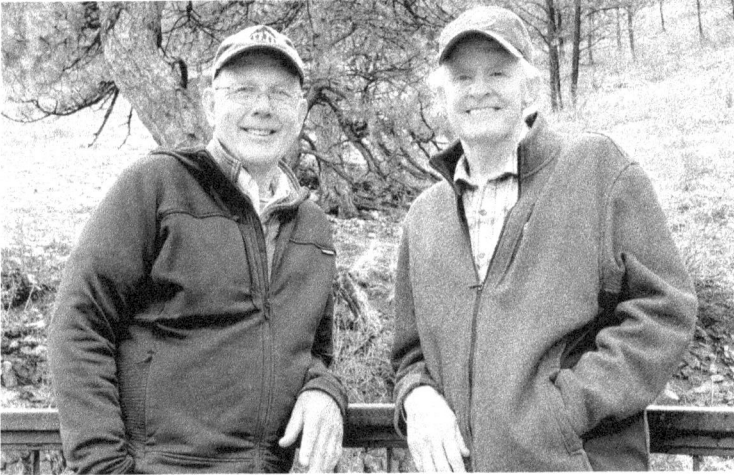

Mike Haddorff (left) and Mike Hamel (right)

Mike Haddorff

I grew up in Fort Collins, Colorado, where I founded, operated for over forty years, and eventually sold an electrical business. I've always had a teacher's mind; it's how I think. At an early age, I was able to develop and exercise this joy within the context of the church. I started teaching at Fort Collins Bible Chapel and today teach at our home church, Council Tree Covenant Church of Fort Collins.

In 2005, entirely out of left field and with the help of some very dear friends, we began Christ in the Rockies. CITR is designed to equip men to live an authentic,

Christ-centered life. CITR pursues this mission by hosting camps for men of all ages in the Colorado Rockies. We also assist others in their efforts to provide outdoor adventure experiences for men of all ages.

I have always loved the outdoors. During this season, one of my interests is fly-fishing, specifically through instructing and guiding others in their journey within the sport. Sandra and I have been married since 1976.

We have four grown children who still like to hang out with Mom and Dad.

Mike Hamel

Born in Kansas and raised in Denver, I served as a teaching pastor in churches in Colorado, Oregon, and Illinois. There, I also directed the Resource Center at Interest Ministries and briefly edited Interest magazine before becoming a freelance writer in 1996. Since then, I've written or substantially edited over forty books on topics as wide-ranging as business, finance, political theory, healthcare, cancer, nonprofits, and religion. These include twenty books for children and young adults.

For the first half of my adult life, I was a preacher. For the second half, I've been a storyteller. I vastly prefer stories to sermons, especially children's stories. Preaching tells hearers what to think and how to act. Storytelling shows readers how characters respond to certain situations and invites consideration.

My wife, Cindy, and I live in Colorado Springs, surrounded by a gaggle of grandkids. You can learn more about me at:

⛰ Christ IN THE Rockies

Seasoned Guides for the Masculine Journey

CITR is a band of brothers who are part of a long tradition of men helping men be men. What we've learned through life experience, including mistakes, we gladly share with others who are on the same masculine journey. We set our event table with the right blend of challenging physical activities and compelling spiritual teaching in the classroom of the great outdoors.

High-adventure outdoor activities are designed for all skill levels and, depending on the camp, can include fly fishing, mountain biking, rock climbing, and rafting. Our in-depth teaching includes a blend of Insights from Scripture, counsel from experts, testimonies from men with unique life experiences, as well as quiet time for personal reflection.

Mountaintop Experiences

We don't live on the mountaintop all the time, but mountaintop experiences can change how we live the rest of the time. Our camps and retreats change lives. Just ask any of the hundreds of men aged 16 to 90 who have attended our events since 2007.

We offer a wide range of camps and retreats specifically crafted for key times in the masculine journey:

- Passage to Manhood camps for fathers and sons
- Going Inward - Moving Onward camps for men 35 and older
- The Way of Wisdom camps for men 50 and older

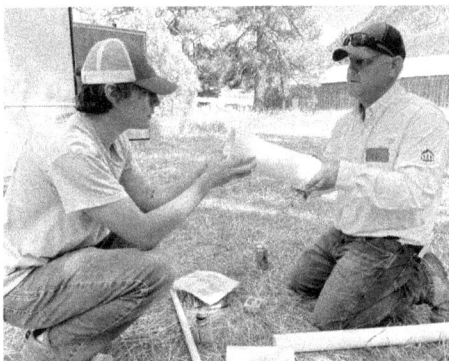

Learn more about Christ in the Rockies, watch alumni testimonials, or sign up for one of our camps here.